6 Weeks to a Great Webinar

*Generate Leads and
Tell Your Story to the World*

by the Greatwebmeetings.com™ Team

6 Weeks to a Great Webinar

Copyright © 2008 Achis Marketing Services

ISBN 978-0-9820377-1-3

TABLE OF CONTENTS

WHAT THE "6 WEEKS TO A GREAT WEBINAR" SYSTEM IS ALL ABOUT

Imagine having the ability to invite everyone you ever wanted to learn about your company or organization hear and see you give that one presentation that would make them customers for a lifetime. Now imagine the nightmare of travel, room reservations and other costs.

THAT'S why webinars are becoming a standard way of marketing and telling the world about your brand. We've helped countless companies do them successfully.

Over the last 5 or 6 years, more and more companies, large and small, are using web presentations to market their products, increase brand awareness, launch products and show the world they are thought leaders. An unscientific study shows that most managers receive 2-3 invitations a week to attend these events. Obviously, when they work, they work well.

But like the proverbial duck in the water, while the good ones appear seamless and calm, there is a lot of paddling that goes on under the surface. And those are the ones that work well - my guess is that you've been on your share of them that didn't. Not only do you not want to attend another webinar from that company, but you don't want to BE that company and fear is preventing you from doing webinars of your own.

This system is designed to help you use checklists and tools to take the guesswork out of putting on your first webinar. If you're an experienced webinar presenter, you'll now have a system so you can do them over and over again.

With this workbook you will learn to:

- Identify who does what, with which, and to whom

- Take a webinar from first ideas to follow-up

- Build a simple project timeline that allows for lots of practice, editing and interruptions from the real world

- Increase the quality of your contact database

- Generate qualified prospects to generate more revenue, faster

- Look like a big player in your field, even if you're a one-person shop

If you're already doing webinars, this will be a great way to identify what's already working for you and improve what isn't. If you're a newbie, you'll avoid many of the common pitfalls and stresses that are endemic to most webinar presentations.

We want to make this process as painless and profitable for you as possible. Have fun and good luck!

The Greatwebmeetings.com™ team

LET'S PUT ON A WEBINAR!

How do you get the word out about your product? How does your company get to demonstrate its thought leadership and get a leg up on bigger competitors? How can you get your message in front of prospects no matter where they are in the world without jet lag and high travel costs?

One answer is to do a webinar. Dozens, hundreds, even thousands of people (if you're Oprah Winfrey) can see and hear your presentation on their computers without you or them leaving their desks. How hard can it be?

The truth is, a successful webinar takes every bit as much thought and work as any other important presentation. What makes it easier, is that there are fewer moving pieces. What makes it tougher is that you're usually using technology you aren't familiar with and the dynamics of a successful web presentation are different than a live face-to-face meeting.

The "6 Weeks to a Great Webinar" system is designed to help you:

- Identify all the components of a great webinar campaign

- Give you the tools to address each stage systematically and track who does what with which and to whom

- Identify what will make your webinar a success - and help you achieve those goals

- Give you everything you need to systematically put on this event - and many more in the future

There are a couple of things we should say before we get started. First, we should define "webinar".

While it is often used to mean any presentation given over the internet via WebEx or LiveMeeting or Dimdim or any of the other 127 web conference providers out there, we are talking specifically about marketing events where you invite prospects and customers from outside your company to learn about a new product, share in your subject expertise on something important to them, or just find out what makes you a good fit to work with them.

We are also assuming that the goals of your webinar are:

- Free to attendees (paid webinars have some subtle but important differences)

- To improve your company's brand awareness

- To generate new leads

- To help expand inside existing customers

- To qualify prospects and move the right customers to the next stage of the sales process

Why are we making these assumptions? Because that's how most successful webinars work. Over the last five years companies have developed a list of best practices and this workbook will share them with you so you can avoid the common mistakes so many people have made before you. Of course, if you're really adventurous you can stumble out on your own, the choice is yours.

WHO ARE YOU TRYING TO REACH?

Before you start building your webinar, you have to answer another important question: Who is the audience for your webinar? More importantly, who is the audience who will take the action you want them to take based on your objectives?

Let me give you an example. If your webinar focuses on what your new servers can do against the competition, it's tempting to think that your audience is the engineers who will use that server. But let me ask you - *are they in a position to buy it or even recommend a demo if that's your goal?*

Which will be more valuable to you - a large audience of end users, or a small audience of people with purchasing and decision power? Only you know the answer to that.

Some of the factors you have to account for are:

- Are you looking at a particular niche market or at a more general audience?

- What level of the organization are you aiming at (senior decision makers, influencers, individual contributors)?

- Who is likely to attend, and what will attract them (senior decision makers like big names and **big picture topics, finance folks want hard data and precise information**)?

- If you could invite your dream audience, who would they be? What would that audience most want to hear from you?

This may be the most important early step you take - this decision will influence who you invite, what the topic should be, and what examples or data you'll use to make your case when you finally build your presentation.

SETTING THE DATE

When do you hold your webinar? If it's a business-to-business webinar you will want to catch people when they are in work mode but not so busy that they won't make time to attend.

The latest research shows the most popular days of the week to hold webinars are Thursday followed by Wednesday. You'll have to decide if you want to hold your event the same time as everyone else.

Additionally, you have to decide if the audience is going to be in one time zone (say only in the UK, or based in a single state of the US) or will have to span time zones. If that's the case you'll probably want to hold your event to span the lunch hours of your audience. This usually means 1 PM Eastern time, which makes it 10 AM on the West Coast of the US.

The only real concerns would be doing it too early on a Monday, or too late on a Friday unless your primary audience is international and you're accommodating their schedules.

Our experience is that people in California or Seattle usually work earlier in the day in order to work with their colleagues in the rest of the country and the world. Depending on what you know about your audience you may opt for something earlier in the day.

If your webinar is aimed at individuals, you might want to get them when they're not on company time. They will probably want to get the dishes done and the kids calmed down, so look at holding it close to 8 or 9 PM, depending on where you are geographically.

Once you've set the date, the clock is ticking.

6 Weeks Out

6 WEEKS TO A GREAT WEBINAR ROLES AND RESPONSIBILITIES

As part of the "6 Weeks to a Great Webinar" system, we throw some job titles and responsibilities around. Just to eliminate confusion this is what we're talking about.

Not to confuse you, but one person might serve in several roles. The **Producer** might also be a **Presenter**, they might be **Support Staff** but they cannot be just a **Sponsor**. We will tell you though that if you're filling more than 3 roles on this checklist, you're working way too hard.

What is critical to remember is - once the task.

Webinar Producer: This is essentially the "project manager" for the webinar. They are involved from the first discussion to the final task. Usually (we recommend it but some find ways to weasel out of it) the producer takes an active role in the webinar itself as well as serves as the point person throughout the planning and follow-up process.

Specific tasks for the producer may include:

- Tracking timelines and tasks for the project

- Setting the audio and visual specs for the recording

- Introducing the presenters on the webinar

- Facilitating the questions during and at the end of the webinar

- Recording and editing the finished version

- Being the point person for questions and communication throughout the process

Webinar Presenter(s): Depending on the type of webinar you're conducting you may have more than one speaker on the presentation. (We'll talk about options later.) These folks should be expert in their field and good presenters. Being a good presenter in a live presentation is no guarantee you'll be a good web presenter, but being a poor presenter in person is pretty a much a sure ticket to a dull webinar.

Because it's important that the presenter be completely comfortable with the content, we suggest that they do most – if not all - of the following tasks:

- Contribute to the creation of the webinar at the early stages (outcomes, objectives, topic)

- Contribute or write all the drafts of the script

- Contribute to the invitation letters

- Contribute to creating the survey questions (if you know what you're being assessed on it's easier to achieve those goals)

- Rehearse like their lives (or at least their careers) depend on it and view the recording of that rehearsal

- Engage the audience and keep your energy level high while presenting

Webinar Sponsor: Inside every organization there is someone ultimately responsible for the success of the webinar and ensuring there are sufficient resources to achieve that success. Additionally, this person will often be uninvolved in the day to day presentation but will be a figurehead on invitations and other communication to prospects and attendees. Depending on the size of your company, this might be your CEO, your VP of Sales or your Head of Marketing. Either way YOU tell them that their role tasks are:

- Assist in assigning roles and responsibilities

- Understand the project timeline and ensure resources (including time) are available

- Be the "big name" on the invitations and promotional material

- Pay for the after-webinar celebration

Support Staff: These are the folks who will do all the things that will make the Producer's life easier. They can be one overworked person or a whole team but this team will:

- Create the PowerPoint or other visuals

- Send out all the invitations

- Monitor databases and attendees

- Update the website with landing page and registrations

- Attend rehearsals and offer honest feedback

- Make the presenters look brilliant

If everyone pulls together and delivers on their tasks, your organization will have not only one successful webinar, but a system that you'll be able to replicate over and over. Good luck and have fun!

CHOOSING A PLATFORM

WebEx, LiveMeeting, Dimdim, LiveConference Pro, Adobe Connect…at last count there were about 127 different providers of web presentation platforms. Some are free (Dimdim) or relatively inexpensive (GoToWebinar) while others are more expensive but have many cool features (WebEx, Adobe Connect). Which one should you choose?

You have to think about your audience as well as your objectives. You want something easy to present with but able to deliver a professional presentation you can be proud of. Below are some of the things you should look for in a platform.

Note that some platforms update their product (and their prices) several times a year so check their website or talk to a customer service rep to make sure the features you want are available and at what price.

COST

Free is better than expensive, right? Well, if your budget is extremely tight, then yes you want to save as much money as you can while still accomplishing your goal. That's the important part - accomplishing your objectives. Just know that with free services you get what you pay for (they all work, but they lack some of the cool features like recording and polling that make these tools powerful). Also know that even the expensive platforms usually charge per connection, meaning that you only pay for the people who actually attend the webinar while it's live. At most you'll pay in the vicinity of 40 cents per person per minute, or for a one-hour webinar, $20 per person. A 100 person webinar will cost you about $2000. Have you priced out the rates for a hotel conference room? And the local Ramada doesn't take pity on you if your attendees don't show.

Additionally you have to decide if you want to use your own data base or purchase a list from a service. This is your prerogative, and the prices range from the inexpensive to the outrageous, depending on the quality of the list. One way to save money here is to partner with another company on the webinar and have them contribute their database as well. Argue it out with your marketing folks over a frosty beverage.

RECORDING

You want to record this event for two reasons. First, you want to have something to post up later on your website to attract prospects in the future and allow those who registered but didn't show up (remember that will be about half) to still get the benefit of your presentation. Plus, when you're in the middle of presenting it's impossible to see what the audience sees and hears. By recording it, you'll see all the ways you can do better next time. It's painful but critical if you're going to constantly improve your webinars.

The more expensive options offer recording as part of their package. Some, like LiveMeeting, will record it as a WMV or Windows Media file. This is a good option because it allows you to edit the final product. Others, like WebEx, will record it in their own proprietary format.

The less expensive options may not allow for recording, although there are alternatives, like recording the webinar with Camtasia or some other similar software. It will depend on the internal expertise of your organization. Are you looking for an all-in-one solution, or do you have someone - even a teenage son or daughter - who is capable of manipulating the files for you?

One thing to pay close attention to: does it record both the AUDIO and the VIDEO? Many platforms record the visuals on the screen but it's tricky to get it to record the audio. If you aren't using a system that uses VOIP (it means the voice goes over the internet and can be heard through your computer speakers as well as, or instead of, the telephone) it might be tricky to configure the audio. Ask your platform provider to demonstrate the set-up. Always test the recording function before settling on a presentation platform!

FIREWALLS AND PLUG-INS

There are two basic types of web presentation platforms- those that require the audience to download software in order to see the presentation (WebEx, LiveMeeting) and those that use Flash and allow them to see the webinar on the web without downloading anything extra.

Basically, here's the deal. The more cool features your webinar has (video, polling, recording,) the more likely they'll require a plug in. These will require that your audience:

1) Download and check it before show time or you'll be delayed

2) Can even use it on their work computers. Many companies, especially financial institutions, have firewalls and blockers that don't allow people to download unauthorized software.

The bottom line here: if you need a robust platform, and you already have a provider like WebEx or LiveMeeting, use what you have. If you need something simple, and your audience is spread out and you're not sure what their firewall situation is, test it out with people outside of your work network before committing to a platform vendor.

OTHER FEATURES TO CONSIDER

Here are some other features you might want to consider:

- Streaming videos and webcams - video isn't all it's cracked up to be but it does help the presenter put a face to a name and as bandwidth increases it becomes easier to use.

- Polling- the most effective webinars engage the audience and make them part of the conversation. A great way to do that is to use polling tools that allow you to create assessment questions and have the audience vote. Some platforms have it, some don't. Some allow you to permanently capture the feedback. This is a really nice feature to have with large webinars when you have to mute everyone's microphone.

- Chat - do you want people to be able to chat and IM each other and the presenter? It's a way of keeping people engaged, it helps capture questions and feedback if you don't have a polling feature or a formal Q and A tool built into the platform. I'm a big fan of this option, but a lot of new presenters are nervous about giving the audience the right to communicate directly with the presenter. It IS distracting at first, but I'm a big believer in treating your audience like adults. Tell them how to use the tool and trust they'll do it.

- Annotation Tools - these give you the ability to mark up your PowerPoint presentation with a highlighter, arrows or other tools. A good set of annotation tools can help spiff up a static presentation when you're on the same slide for too long- look for one that allows you to change the color so it complements your PowerPoint color scheme.

- Desktop and Application Sharing - Does your webinar involve going to your website or demonstrating what your software does? Your platform should allow you to easily share your desktop or the application with your audience with one or two clicks of a mouse, and not have to slow down your whole show to do it

- Invitation process - does the webinar have a method for inviting large blocks of people without displaying everyone's e-mail address? Almost as important, does it allow you to create a reminder in Outlook so that they automatically block the time in their schedules. This will increase your attendance and reduce confusion over time zones

It's important that you choose your platform, then build your presentation to make the most of it.

6 WEEKS TO A GREAT WEBINAR CHECKLIST

Purpose	To identify all the roles and tasks associated with putting on a great webinar
Who Should Use	Webinar producer, presenter(s) and support staff
Roles and Tasks	Webinar Topic: Webinar Presenter: Webinar Producer: Webinar Title: Webinar Date: Webinar Sponsor: Webinar Support Staff:

6 Weeks

❏ Agree on desired outcomes

❏ Determine Topic

❏ Determine Speaker

❏ Determine Producer

❏ Set Date and Time

❏ Investigate platforms

5 Weeks

❏ Get your data bases together

❏ Review Call to Action

❏ Determine title

❏ Determine data to be captured during registration

❏ Premiums and special offers

4 Weeks

- ❏ Finalize platform choice
- ❏ Schedule webinar in platform
- ❏ Create Landing Page for your website
- ❏ First invitation draft to stakeholders
- ❏ Draft of Registration Confirmation letter
- ❏ Script outline

3 Weeks

- ❏ 1st invitations sent out
- ❏ First draft of script to stakeholders

2 Weeks

- ❏ 2nd Invitation* goes out
- ❏ "Pretty close to final" script done

10 Days

- ❏ Plan evaluation survey
- ❏ Plan questions for Q and A
- ❏ Rehearsal!
- ❏ Edit, argue, finalize
- ❏ Premiums finished?

1 Week

- ❏ 3rd* round of invites
- ❏ Cycling slides*
- ❏ Reminder letter goes out

- ❏ Create "Thank You for Joining Us" letter

- ❏ Create "Sorry You Weren't There" letter

4 Days

- ❏ Dress Rehearsal

- ❏ Feedback and late changes

1 Day

- ❏ Final reminder notice goes out

- ❏ Final tech test (recording)

Show Day!

- ❏ Present your webinar

- ❏ Follow up with evaluations, premiums

1 Day After

- ❏ "Sorry You Weren't There" letter

- ❏ "Thank You for Joining Us" letter

- ❏ Check evaluations

- ❏ Post recording on your website

- ❏ Get leads to sales people

After that

- ❏ Debrief with the team

- ❏ Celebrate your success!

5 WEEKS OUT

DATA BASES AND LISTS

If you're going to throw a party, one of the first questions you'd ask is: "Who should we invite?" This is even more true of webinars - after all your goal is to not only throw the biggest party possible, but invite as many people who don't know you well as you can in order to grow your business.

Now is the time to look at what you have and what you need. If you already have an extensive list of prospects, like an e-mail list or a subscription to your newsletter, that's a great start. Of course, not all businesses have great lists. If you only have a few hundred people in your e-mail data base, you're not going to have a big attendance, but if they're the right people, they CAN drive business.

There are two ways to instantly expand the scope of your invitations, and you need to make these decisions right now:

1) Partner with someone (a vendor, a subject matter expert in your industry) who has their own (preferably larger) list. Many successful webinars are hosted by companies who simply present experts from all kinds of areas to their audience and achieve their ends by being associated with better known names.

2) Buy a list. Be very careful, however. As with any marketing list, you have to make sure you are buying the most carefully targeted and accurate list possible. If your audience is made up of Chief Information Officers, make sure your list isn't full of solo IT consultants and hardware geeks, or individual contributors with little influence on buying decisions.

This issue of targeting is important, but you have to be realistic. You want to invite the people who are most interested in the topic AND can help you achieve your objectives. However, if your data base isn't quite that sophisticated, don't worry. This is your first webinar, and as we go along you'll have a way of breaking out information so you can be smarter and more effective the next time.

You'll need a week or more to get a good list together so start now.

CALL TO ACTION REVIEW

Before you start to build your presentation or send out your invitations, can you state in once sentence (two if you must) what your presentation is going to accomplish:

As the presenting company?

At the end of this presentation, I want the audience to:

As an audience member?

At the end of the presentation, I want to know/learn/understand/do:

This is one of those things that is easy to say, and hard to do but here it goes: from now on, everything you put into your invitation, webinar content and follow-up should:

• Help accomplish your goals as the presenting company

• Be relevant to the audience's desired outcome

You'd be surprised if you use this as your filter, how much content won't fit into your presentation. Lots of cool "value added" information will be excluded (good, save it for Q and A), supporting data and numbers (your audience will thank you, trust me. If they need it they'll ask).

GET A WORKING TITLE

"What's in a name?," asked the poet. The answer is, pretty much everything.

Your prospective audience has a lot going on, and you need to invite them to an event that will give them maximum value for the investment of their time.

Think about how you read your e-mail - you look at the subject line, maybe read the first paragraph in the preview pane and either open it or delete it. Most often you delete it. You want something that is going to grab them and make them interested in what you have to offer. Ironically, it won't be anything about you.

Read that again, **it's not about you**. People will read e-mail, register, and make time for only something that has benefit to them, so the title of your webinar is very important. Don't believe us?

Let's say one of your most pressing business problems is the invasion of the Lithuanian Boll Weevil

"_____ *introduces our Boll Weevil killer.*" Well, unless the reader knows who you are, this is about you, not them.

"*Solving the Lithuanian Boll Weevil problem with* _____*'s new bug spray.*" Okay, they have a Boll Weevil problem but this is going to be a non-stop commercial for one product. Maybe it's worth it, maybe not.

"*Five ways to solve the Lithuanian Boll Weevil problem, brought to you by* _____." There are 5 ways to fight this problem? Who knew? They might learn something…it's even worth sitting through the commercial for.

The additional advantage of identifying the title early, is it forces you to focus your message. Are there 5 ways to fight this bug? What would they be? You'll identify most of the components of your presentation before you even start to write it…anything to beat writer's block!

CAPTURE THE DATA!

While the content of your webinar is important, the main purpose for doing it is to expand your reach beyond your current data base and marketing efforts. Remember, when people sign up for a webinar, even if they don't show up (and we'll say it again, free webinars have about a 50% no-show rate) they have expressed an interest in the topic. That's already better than a cold call.

It's critical to capture as much information as you can without scaring people off. Most good registration systems will have both required data and as much information as people want to volunteer.

Whether you're using a landing page on your website (the best idea) or the platform's system, you need information you can immediately follow up on, as well as contact information for future marketing and communication. Whether some of this information is important to you depends on your sales or marketing strategy. Do your divide sales territory by industry? By geography? Who in the organization do you sell to?

Required Information

At the very least you should require:

- Name

- E-mail Address (many people will use a generic account like Gmail or Hotmail or a personal e-mail address to avoid being hunted down at work. They don't know you very well, do they?)

- Position in their company (assuming it's a business related webinar, not aimed at individuals)

"Really Nice to Have" Information

These will make your follow-up and future prospecting events much easier if people will voluntarily give you:

- Phone Number

- Company or Organization

- Work E-mail

- City

In this era of electronic connection, physical address is less important than nailing their location down to who they work for and the city they work in. The minute you ask for mailing address people will assume you'll send them junk mail and hunt them down where they live. Don't arouse unnecessary suspicions.

PREMIUMS FOR ATTENDEES

The primary goal of your webinar is to get as many people to register for your event as possible - after all you're about getting the contact information for the future as much as anything else. Still, you want people to attend once they've registered since that will push them farther along the sales cycle.

One way to encourage people to attend once they've registered is to offer a premium for actual attendance, not just registering. (Premium is such a nice word compared to "bribe").

The reason you have to decide this now, is you'll be crafting your invitation soon, and you have to know what you're going to offer your audience.

The premium should be something that

- You can afford (and will depend on how many people you realistically expect to attend)

- That has real value to your audience

- Makes you look professional

Adds to the strength of your call to action

Some of the kinds of things that make good premiums are:

- Reprints of magazine articles you've written or been featured in

- White papers that demonstrate subject matter expertise that's important to your customers and reinforce the message of the webinar

- Electronic copies of any books you've written

- PDF copies of the PowerPoint files

- A complimentary assessment or analysis (as opposed to a sales call) with someone from your company

What will your customers want AND will help cement your brand in their mind?

5 WEEKS OUT: WEBINAR PLANNING TOOL

Webinar Name

_____

Stated Objectives

_____

Presenter(s)

_____

Introduction and Housekeeping (3 minutes total)

- Welcome, names of presenters

- Topic, expected outcomes, logistics including how long they'll be on

- Introduce technology, get them to try chatting, polling etc

Agenda and Polling/Assessment (2 minutes total)

- Introduce exact agenda for webinar

- Ask a polling or assessment question (depending on platform used)

Content (approximately 35 minutes)

- You'll want to use an inductive approach for most audiences

- What conclusions do you want them to draw?

- Why is it important to them?

- What evidence do you have (including your product or service)?

- Fulfill your promise to the audience for quality information

- Quick recap and ask for questions

Q and A (10-12 minutes)

You really want to encourage questions…this will give you a chance to remove objections, go deeper into the details than you could in the main body of your presentation and help you explain anything that could be confusing or get in the way of moving the sale forward.

- Explain how you'll take questions

- Start with planted questions to get the ball rolling

- Tie all your answers to your desired outcomes

Wrap-up and Call to Action

This is your call to action…why you're putting yourself through this. You'd be surprised how many presenters try to "wing it" or try to close too fast and forget to specifically tell the audience what the next step is.

- Summarize your main points

- Repeat action item(s)

- Thank presenters/partners as appropriate

- Remind the audience about the recording, tell their friends, fill out the evaluation form

4 WEEKS OUT

SCHEDULE YOUR WEBINAR

It's now 4 weeks before Webinar Day. It's time to schedule your webinar. Why? Because most platforms create a unique ID for the event and you'll want to include it in your press releases, invitations and e-mail signatures.

When setting your webinar up, make sure you

- Designate who will be presenter(s)

- Block out the time for 15 minutes before and 15 minutes after the actual webinar time

- Heck, while you're at it, schedule the rehearsals and get them on everyone's calendar so they can't find excuses

Make sure that the event is tied to people's Outlook or Gmail calendars if your platform provider has that option.

This is real; it's happening and time for everyone to hit those milestones to make this webinar a big success.

FINALIZE YOUR PLATFORM CHOICE

It's time to quit arguing, dithering and sweating it out. If you haven't yet chosen a platform for your webinar…do it now.

You can't build your presentation, send out your invitations or finalize a date until you have this decision made.

There, don't you feel better?

YOUR LANDING PAGE AND DATA CAPTURE

When people are deciding to attend a webinar, they do it on the basis of:

- Is the content worth my while?

- Do the presenters have credibility and expertise?

- Is it going to be a hassle to sign up or view the event?

Remember, your invitation is designed to be read in the preview pane of their e-mail. To give all the detail you want, you should have a dedicated page on your website that they can visit.

All the invitations will link to it, so your prospects will be able to check you out and easily register

It will be linked to your home page so people coming across your website will also find out about the webinar, even if they weren't on your radar.

Make the page look professional. Pictures of the presenters, your company's logo and maybe a preview of some of the content will help encourage people to attend.

It will capture the information you need for this and future events. Remember they will volunteer this information in exchange for the value you'll bring them. If possible, have the registration form/data capture on the same page. Every time your audience has to click to give you information there's a chance you'll lose them.

Use the questions back on the Data Capture Criteria page to plan your form. Which information will be required, and which will be "nice to have".

Test the page, and make sure the information is exporting to your contact files before offering it live to the world.

This is it, you're ready to invite people to your webinar.

FIRST INVITATION DRAFT (TO STAKEHOLDERS)

Your invitations go out into the world next week. Now is the time to craft it and make sure that all your stakeholders are happy with it. Remember, it has to be pitch-perfect as this will be your first impression on your prospects.

The 6 Weeks To a Great Webinar system will have 3 invitations in total, so this is not your only shot at your audience.

Stakeholders will include:

- The Webinar Sponsor - who in your organization has final authority for external messages? It might be the President, the VP of Marketing or the Product Manager

- The Producer, Presenter(s) and anyone who's working on the webinar script - you want to make sure what they're building and planning to present matches what you're inviting people to attend

- Internal resources with a stake in success (if you don't let your Sales or Business Development people take a look at the invitation before it goes out, you're inviting drama afterwards).

- Someone with good proof-reading skills who hasn't already seen the message 18 times. Trust me there's something wrong with what you think is your final draft, but you've read it too often to see it. Let a fresh set of eyes go over your document.

A good invitation does 5 things:

1) 1.Catches the eye of the reader in the e-mail invitation

2) 2.Calls attention to something of concern to the audience - usually a pressing business need

3) 3.Tells the audience how attending your webinar will help them address that need

4) 4.Gives them all the relevant logistical information and makes it easy to register

5) 5.Allows them to opt out of your mailing list (but don't make it too easy)

Send the first draft to anyone who might feel they have a stake in the outcome…you want to spot any errors as well as make sure everyone's onboard with the event.

SAMPLE E-MAIL INVITATION

This invitation assumes that your audience is more interested in the topic than who is presenting it. Unless you are a well-known industry leader you might want to take this approach - after all most people you send this to will have no idea who you are - yet!

Subject Line: 5 Ways to stop Lithuanian Boll Weevils - new webinar

Body: Lithuanian Boll Weevils are the number one business problem for farmers. Did you know there are 5 things you can do immediately to protect your farm and stop this pest in its tracks?

Join us on _____ at _____ for a free webinar: "5 Things You Can Do Right Now To Stop Lithuanian Boll Weevils." (Presenters) of (your company) will give you practical advice on protecting your investment and solving one of the most challenging problems in your business.

Register now by clicking here. (This links to your landing/data capture page)

In this webinar you'll learn:

(Insert your learning objectives here)

ADDED BONUS: Besides this valuable practical information, attendees will receive _____.

About The Presenters: Include 2 sentence bio(s) of your presenter(s)

About your company

Don't forget to join us (date and time) for this important event.

Register here (repeat link to landing/data capture page).

Personalized signature of Someone Important

(President, CEO, Chief Marketing Officer)

Contact information and website info

We respect your privacy. To take your name off our e-mail list, please click here (e-mail link) and put REMOVE in the subject line.

DRAFT OF REGISTRATION CONFIRMATION LETTER

This letter is almost as important as the invitation. It is designed to be sent out immediately upon registration (your contact software or webmaster might automate this, but small companies can do this by hand if they have to).

This letter should accomplish several things:

- Thank participants for registering (your mother raised you right)

- Reinforce the value they will receive from attending (you want them to remember to show up)

- Give them the critical data to log in and connect (you'll have to do this again, people forget)

- Allow them to test for connectivity or download plug-ins prior to the event (critical, although many won't bother and some folks will not be able to connect, you can only control what you can control)

- (if possible) Automatically put the date on their calendars (prevents time zone confusion and overbooking)

- Encourage them to invite others (after all, you want to reach out to as many people as possible…let your prospects market for you as well)

Send this letter out to all stakeholders for proofing and buy-in. Do it now, the invitations go out in a couple of days and people will start registering.

TEST THE PLATFORM...NOW...WE'RE NOT KIDDING

If you haven't used the presentation platform you've chosen yet, the time is now. The rest of your timeline depends on the functionality of the platform you've chosen (and this is where some of the investment in the more robust platforms starts to pay off).

Here are the questions to answer and things to test:

- Does it require a plug-in? (If so, let your audience know that when they get the invitation as well as details and links to load it ahead of showtime)

- Will it work across firewalls and different networks? (Don't just try it with someone in your office, try it at a Starbucks, try it from home. If you have a colleague in a foreign country, get them to help you for 5 minutes. You need to know NOW what problems people might have joining your webinar so you can mitigate them).

- What features does it have and how will you use them? (Do you know how the polling works? Can you share applications easily? How will you use that feature in your presentation (or will you use it?)

- Test the recording feature. Make sure you document how to get sound and audio working together. The day before the webinar is not the time for experimentation. You want to plan this webinar with the future in mind...having it up on your website is an important follow-up step.

- How does the invitation system work? Here are the things you'll need to figure out before you send out your invitations:

  ° Can you just use your current bulk e-mail tool (Constant Contact, for example)

  ° Does the webinar platform provide an automatic e-mail tool? (Most of the big brands do.)

  ° Is there a way to automatically schedule the event in peoples' calendars (Outlook and Google Calendar are the most common applications, and for work it's Outlook).

- Do a test and make sure you're comfortable with how everything works and how an invitation will look to the receiver.

Now you know what the thing will do, what features you'll incorporate into your presentation and how you'll invite people to attend in a way that makes you look professional.

SCRIPT OUTLINE TOOL

Many people make the mistake of building their presentation as they go. We think the easiest way to be successful is to build the frame and then put the meat on it - this sheet will help.

Remember you are aiming to do a 1 hour webinar (which will probably be 55 minutes total, because the next webinar that starts on time will be the first to ever accomplish that feat.) The skeleton of the presentation looks roughly like this:

Introduction and housekeeping 3 Minutes

Agenda, introductory polling or audience assessment 2 Minutes

The main content of your presentation 35-40 minutes

Q and A 10-12 minutes

Wrapup and call to action 3 Minutes

You'll notice that leaves you about 35 minutes for the content of your presentation. This might not seem like a long time, but remember some of your possible objectives:

- You're not trying to close a sale right there, you're trying to get them excited enough to schedule a demo

- You don't want to teach them everything about the topic, you want them to attend future live events or trainings

Can you teach them everything they need to know in 35 minutes? Probably not but you CAN convince them that you and your team know enough that they'll want to do business with you and THAT is the reason you are putting yourself through this misery. Remembering that will help when you have to cut the "really cool" parts out of your presentation.

Basically the outline looks like this:

Introduction and Housekeeping

- Who are you, who is presenting and what are you talking about?

- Are they familiar with the interface? Do they know how to ask questions, use the voting or chat features? Help them get comfortable with the technology

- How will you take questions (chat, Q and A feature, by voice or written) and will the chat feature be open

- What's expected of them? (participation, questions, polling, shut off e-mail - really)

Agenda, introductory polling and audience assessment

- What's the agenda for the presentation (including how much time it will take)

- Get to know the audience (one or two polling questions)

Polling does several important things in helping achieve your objectives. You might want to make sure you're talking to the right level of the organization. Can these people make a final decision or are they going to have to convince their bosses? What do you have to change to make your presentation as relevant to your audience as possible?

By voting, they have started to pay you more attention and now have a stake in the presentation…it's time to deliver on your promise….

If you don't have a true fancy polling option on your platform, you can still ask your audience to vote yes or no by either using the chat box or by using the feedback mechanism (Dimdim, for example offers a "thumbs up" or "thumbs down" option).

Think of the information you'd like most to gain from your audience:

- Level of the organization

- Biggest business challenges

- Level of interest in your topic

Each of these will help you tailor your presentation and start to qualify your prospects. Plus by participating you've built in a way for them to have a stake in the outcome. Your webinar will be more engaging and thus more effective in getting to your objectives!

The Content

You'll want to deliver your content in a way that is clear and drives to your outcome. In order to do this, we suggest you start with an inductive, rather than a deductive approach. That sounds more complicated than it is - although some of the more analytical among us will have heart palpitations.

Here it is in a nutshell: rather than start slowly and build to a conclusion, you start with your conclusion and then support it. So, instead of "here are all the reasons hiring people is so difficult so it's why you need to use assessment tools (and preferably ours)", you would say "assessment tools are critical to today's hiring managers, here's why." The difference may sound minor but by taking this approach, you'll do a couple of things:

- Answer the audience's primary question- "what's this about and where is the presenter going?"

- Many presenters try to "make a strong case" before giving their recommendation - but the tendency is to overload the presentation with data and thus make it too long and dry for the audience.

- You're not fooling your audience. They know there will be a blatant sales pitch somewhere…it's why you're doing this free webinar. The hard part is giving them sufficient value in exchange for their time that they won't mind.

Questions and Answers

You'll want to build time into your presentation for a robust Q and A session. Interested people ask questions and that's where most sales are made. Figure out early on how you'll take questions…by voice? Written in a formal Q and A box ? In the Chat window???

Wrap-up and Call to Action

Your closing should do several things:

- Thank them for their time

- Summarize your main points

- Reinforce the value you've brought to the audience

- Tell them exactly what the next steps are

This outline will help you plan your presentation before sitting down and agonizing over PowerPoint or trying to start from a blank page.

3 WEEKS OUT

SEND OUT INVITATIONS

Take a deep breath. It's time to send out your e-mail invitations. This is it…..

Once you have hit send, a couple of things will occur:

- You'll immediately panic and second guess yourself. Just breathe.

- You will start to get e-mail responses…lots of them.

- Check your e-mail, see how many bounced-back messages you get

    ° Every time you get a bounced back message examine it and take action:

    ° Check if there was a mistake in the address (anyone@homail instead of hotmail)

    ° If the e-mail is not mistyped but bounces back, go IMMEDIATELY and delete that customer from your data base. One of the most important things about your first webinar is to create a solid base for future marketing. Bad e-mail addresses are a waste of time and energy.

    ° Remove people who wish to unsubscribe immediately. The last thing you want is to be known as a spammer

    ° If you know the person the invitation went to but it bounced back, take that as a reason to reach out to them by phone or in person. You need to have this information for the future plus you'll personally extend the invitation to them - odds are better they'll attend.

YOUR FIRST DRAFT OF THE SCRIPT

Yes, we said script. Remember, you need to know how long your presentation is, and your stakeholders are going to want to check out your content before the first rehearsal.

The best way to do this is to use the "notes" section in PowerPoint. (We are assuming that, like 90% of companies you'll be using this to create your visuals). The advantage this gives you is when you print your slides and notes out, you have a perfect script for presenting from. Yes, it's early, and most people wouldn't ask you to have your first draft done yet, but we are trying to cut trouble off at the pass.

Especially with your first webinar, your stakeholders will all have something to say about your presentation. Give them the opportunity to buy-in. Your first draft does not have to be perfect, but it does have to have all the important components:

- Show the beginning to end arc of the presentation. (Does it cover all the salient points?)

- Demonstrate where you'll have interactive components. (polling, questions)

- Have the important graphs and visuals. (Someone might have questions or have a better visual somewhere. Give them a chance to provide it and make your life easy.)

- Have the script to the point where all stakeholders know what you're going to say and check it for clarity and accuracy.

While in your final draft, you don't want your script written out word for word (you'll be tempted to read it, believe us), but in this draft your script will have to be complete enough that people know what you're going to say. Just to say "tell the bear story" won't help those unfamiliar with that story and, more importantly, won't help you be concise and clear.

When you are done with your final draft, you will print out every page of your script so that you have a paper copy of your presentation with all the major points, as well as the transition to the next slide and any notes to yourself about the presentation ("annotate this slide with the highlighter", "pause for effect" or "make sure to check that polling results are visible to the audience")

This copy is what you will present from when the time comes.

Here's what the script page looks like in PowerPoint:

Notice all the bold parts? Those are notes to yourself.

In later versions you'll reduce the script to bullet points, but for now you want to put your thoughts on the page.

A WORD ABOUT STORIES

Entertaining, relevant stories and examples are the key to an engaging presentation, and we hope you have lots of great stories, the kind you tell your customers all the time. Here are some differences when presenting on the web:

- You need to be engaging, but the audience can't see your funny facial expressions, keep it short

- Keep the stories on topic and relevant to the presentation. If it doesn't help achieve your outcome, save it for the sales call afterwards

A good example story has three components. Plan your story and put it in your script this way:

1) What was the customer problem or situation

2) What did you do to solve the problem (briefly and precisely)

3) What was the result for the customer

We don't want to take your personal style out of the presentation, but remember these people aren't across a table from you, and you have less time to engage them and prove you are the expert(s).

Send this copy out to your stakeholders and tell them they have a week to get back to you with feedback. Be clear that this is an early draft. If they have a problem with something, ask for specific changes. IF they don't like a visual, ask if they have a better one or a good idea where you can get it.

Finally, if they snooze, they lose. We're on a deadline here.

NOTE TO THE PRODUCER - you are going to get a lot of input. Some of it will be valuable, some of it will be nonsense, and some will be things to think about. You are the final decision maker. That's why you make the big bucks.

2 WEEKS OUT

2 WEEKS OUT SECOND INVITATION*

The reason that this title has an asterisk is that you have a choice to make. While the "6 Weeks to a Great Webinar System" recommends 3 rounds of e-mail invitations, some companies are worried about being perceived as too pushy or winding up listed as spam. This is your call to make. You might skip this invitation and go to the third one, a week before the event.

You don't want to send this invitation to people who have already registered (they have already responded to the first one AND received a registration confirmation. You don't want to be a pest.)

It wouldn't make much sense to send the same invitation that got ignored the last time. Since most people will decide whether they are interested or not in the preview pane of their e-mail box, the two things that should be different in this invitation are the subject line and the first paragraph.

There are a couple of things you can try:

- Stress the urgency of the topic

- Give them a preview of content

Here's an example of a different subject line:

4 of 5 Farmers will have Lithuanian Boll Weevil Problems - new webinar explains

Or

Boll Weevils - Your biggest challenge

And then the first paragraph will engage their interest and make them feel that life as they know it will be lessened by not attending your webinar:

"According to the Farm Labor Bureau, 4 out of 5 farmers will lose crops to these terrible pests this year. Attend our webinar, "5 Ways to Solve the Lithuanian Boll Weevil Problem" and learn from the industry's leading experts how to protect your crops.

The rest of the invitation can be the same.

Don't forget to have this invitation proof-read by someone outside your team.

If you decide to do only two rounds of invitations, congratulations, you've got the second one done already.

"PRETTY CLOSE TO FINAL" DRAFT FINISHED

Once you have received feedback from your stakeholders (and successfully not yelled at anyone, right?), it's time to polish the script. Here are the things to look for:

- Do you have your main points bullet-pointed or at least in short phrases?

- Do you have the transition statement to move to the next slide written out? (This will avoid awkward umms and errrs during the webinar)

- Have you bolded or underlined the things that need special emphasis in your performance?

- Is your call to action clear and written out so you cannot possibly forget it?

You'll probably be making notes and changes right up until the last minute but your script should be in shape to do your first dress rehearsal.

Here's your next step:

Print out the "notes" pages, one page per sheet. You can do it in black and white or grayscale to save ink and stop your office manager from yelling at you.

Use a 3-hole punch and put the script in a binder. This will be your touchstone for the presentation to come.

You're ready for rehearsal!

10 DAYS OUT

PLAN YOUR EVALUATION SURVEY

Since the odds are you're planning to do more webinars in the future, you want to capture audience feedback. What worked well? What didn't work? More importantly, how effective were you in getting your message across?

Here's what you have to keep in mind about your evaluations:

- They must answer the questions you care about most.

- They must go out to the audience immediately after the webinar. The longer the delay, the fewer responses you'll get.

- They must be easy for the audience to fill out.

- They must be short. More than 5 or 6 questions will scare people off.

Even with all this, if you get half the attendees responding, you've done a great job.

While you can certainly put your survey in the form of an e-mail and ask people to respond, by far the most cost, and time, effective method is to use an online survey system. These will not only format your questions and make you look slick, they will organize the information into simple reports that actually make sense.

There are several reputable free (if you ask fewer than 10 questions) or low-cost survey tools out there. Some of them are:

www.surveymonkey.com

www.zoomerang.com

www.freeonlinesurveys.com

www.surveygizmo.com

Most of these tools allow even the most inexperienced user to quickly format an effective post-webinar survey. Once it's complete, you'll receive a unique URL that allows someone to click right into the survey through their web browser. Just put it in a quick e-mail and send it to all attendees the moment the webinar is finished.

Remember, the fewer steps the audience has to take, the more likely you'll get the information you need.

Most tools will allow you to ask your questions in different formats; true-false, yes-no, 1-5 scales. At this stage the numbers are less important than the information you gain. You'll also want to offer them the opportunity to make comments, but don't be insulted if they don't take you up on it. Most people will want to do the bare minimum and move on. Only the very motivated (the raving fans and the really upset) will take a lot of time on the feedback.

Over time you (or your folks in marketing) will want to get more sophisticated but for now your needs are pretty simple.

Here are some of the high-impact questions you'll want answers to:

- Did they find the time well spent? Why or why not?

- Was the presenter effective?

- Was it easy to register and attend? (You always have the right to get smarter as you go.)

- Did you present information they weren't familiar with?

- How likely are they to take action? Would they be willing to take a call? Schedule a demo?

- Would they attend another webinar?

- Would they recommend this webinar to their friends?

If you get the answers to these questions you'll know what you can do better next time, if you hit the mark and if you will get a return on your investment. That's pretty good information.

Create your survey, get the URL and craft your e-mail to attendees, thanking them for attending. There's one less thing you have to think about as show day draws near.

PLANNED (AND PLANTED) QUESTIONS

Have you ever been at a meeting where the speaker says, "I'll take questions now", and the silence is ominous? Now imagine your webinar. You've made your presentation, you have called for action and ask for questions and…nothing. Silence. Your momentum comes to a screeching halt.

Planning 2 or 3 questions in advance will serve a couple of purposes:

- It will allow you to move seamlessly and professionally from the "presentation" into Q and A

- You will be able to answer the questions smoothly (because you know they're coming and you've already planned your answers) and get your feet under you before you take less controllable questions from the audience. Confidence is critical to a successful presentation

- You will be able to edit your presentation better and keep it shorter, if some of the detail that you want to go into will be addressed during Q and A

- You give the audience time to think about their questions. There is also a psychological factor at play…few people want to ask the first question, even if they're bursting for more information. By taking a couple of planted questions first you can remove that barrier AND give them time to ask their questions.

- You position them in the way that works best to achieving your desired outcomes. Rather than ask, "so what does the software cost?" You can ask, "What's the return on investment for this product?"

Planning your questions at this point in the process makes sense for one major reason: You get a chance to rehearse taking questions during your practice sessions. This will help both your confidence and your timing.

Here are the questions to ask yourself at this point of the planning stage:

- What are the 2 or 3 questions you know your audience will ask?

- What information will most help achieve your objectives?

- What question do you dread, but know they'll ask about and how can you rephrase it so it's less scary?

EDIT, ARGUE AND FINALIZE

You've tried your presentation. Your stakeholders have checked it out, you've had innocent eyes look at it and evaluate it for timing, presentation quality and effectiveness. Now is the time to come as close to a final draft as possible. Take the best ideas you've heard and don't be afraid to use them - after all those folks are all on your team and have a stake in the successful outcome. (It doesn't hurt that if you are seen to incorporate their suggestions and occasionally replace your own, you'll get their buy-in and support internally.)

We know you'll be making notes and changes right up until the last minute but the time has come to nail this presentation down.

Print out the notes pages in black and white.

Put them in a three-ring binder.

Your presentation is ready. You're ready…

YOUR FIRST REAL REHEARSAL

Rehearsal for an event as important and expensive as a webinar is NOT:

- Flipping through the slides muttering to yourself

- Leaving huge blanks with "and then we'll say yada yada".

- Done with just the presenters and producer

What this rehearsal IS:

- A chance to do the webinar in the platform you'll be using on show day, using all the tools just as you will during the presentation.

- A chance to do the script pretty close to word-for-word. Is it too long? Too short?

- An opportunity to use the polling, annotation and interactive tools and become familiar with them

- A chance for someone who hasn't obsessed about this presentation for 4 weeks already to hear it and check your message for clarity and offer feedback

- A chance to record it and see what the audience sees and hears. It might be painful but it's invaluable.

- An opportunity to take at least the pre-planned questions and practice short, precise answers to the most important questions your audience will have

Give yourself at least 30 minutes more than your presentation will take. New presenters will have to familiarize themselves with the platform and its tools.

Once you start the presentation, run through it in as close to real time as possible.

Take all the feedback graciously, listen to the recording and decide what you'll do better next time.

Compare notes with the other presenter(s). You might have to make another draft of the script, you might just scribble some notes on your existing script, it all depends on how rehearsal goes.

Can you feel the excitement?

ARE YOUR PREMIUMS DONE?

This one shouldn't take long if everyone has been holding up their end of the bargain. You have promised your attendees they'll receive something of value (in addition to your expertise and the chance to learn about you!) In exchange for their time. Be prepared to honor that promise as quickly as possible.

Make sure it's proofed, completed and in the hands of whoever will be sending it out.

For most small companies, the easiest way to live up to this promise is to e-mail the attendees with the premium attached as soon as they have lived up to their end of the bargain. Send it out with a short note of thanks and an offer to be of service, along with your website and contact info.

You made a promise; you'll deliver on it. Even when the webinar is over you still live up to your promises. This says a lot to prospects.

If your webmaster/mistress is particularly skillful, a nice way to drive your business forward is to have the premium sitting on your website and send the "thank you" e-mail with a code to download the premium from there. This will drive them to your website one more time (you never know what they'll discover) and you'll weed out those who aren't really interested - a nice way to qualify your leads.

1 WEEK OUT

THE THIRD* INVITATION

Whether you're sending 3 or only 2 rounds of invitations, there's only one week until your webinar. By now you should have gotten a lot of responses to your invitation, but you should always be adding names to your list and you never know when someone will change their mind and decide to see what you have to offer. This is really your last opportunity to ramp up the numbers.

This invitation should:

- Have yet another, more urgent subject line

- Have a first paragraph with new, startling information

- Stress that time and space are limited (technically true even if the odds of you exceeding that capacity are slim)

- NOT be sent to people who have already registered. You don't want to pester those folks

Here's a sample. Understand that your organization can decide on the right tone and information appropriate for your brand. Just know this is no time for subtlety.

Sample Subject Line: Boll Weevils- How Much Time Do You Have Left to Fight?

First Paragraph: This year, almost $5 Million dollars in crops will be lost to the Lithuanian Boll Weevil. Do You know how to fight it? Join _____ and dozens of other concerned farmers on their webinar, "5 Ways to Solve the Lithuanian Boll Weevil Crisis"

Don't get discouraged if your first webinar doesn't draw as many people as you'd like. Remember, the goal is to draw in qualified prospects. If you get a dozen prospects but half of them move to the next step in your sales cycle, you're ahead of the game.

CYCLING SLIDES*

When people log onto your webinar (hopefully 15 minutes early, but likely mere seconds before and sometimes after the scheduled start time) what will they see? As we'll discuss, they should at least see your title slide to ensure them they're in the right meeting.

Some of the more robust platforms (Adobe Connect, WebEx, LiveMeeting and others) have an additional feature that will help you look professional and help avoid technology complaints from your audience. It's called "slide cycling" (or some other similar term depending on the platform). What it means is that there is a short set of PowerPoint visuals that are automatically shown and advanced on a loop.

These usually are visible to the audience 15 – 20 minutes before the scheduled start time and are replaced with the actual presentation visuals just as the webinar is about to begin. Set the slides to advance every 15 seconds.

3-4 slides is all that's required. We suggest:

1) The title of the webinar as well as your company's logo

2) A slide with the telephone number and passcode (along with special directions like 'make sure you hit pound after the passcode.') This will help avoid panicky questions about audio problems

3) A picture and short bio of the presenter(s)

4) A phone number to call if they have problems connecting (usually your platform provider but sometimes the tech person in your office serves that role)

THE REMINDER LETTER

You know what it's like…you say you'll do something three weeks from now, but life gets in the way? That same thing happens to your audience. Despite their best intentions, those "urgent but not important" things will take their attention off your event.

One problem with free webinars, is people treat them as if they're worth what they paid for the event. Don't be insulted, just get proactive.

One week before the event, send a short e-mail to everyone who has registered. This will be redundant for many attendees so keep it short. If, on the other hand, you don't have a way of automatically putting this event into their calendars, this can be the difference between a successful event and a great deal of frustration. Don't give them an excuse not to remember your event!

This letter should:

- Thank them for registering

- Confirm their good judgment in agreeing to come

- Reiterate the time and date (with Outlook and Gmail scheduling if you have it)

- Let them test their computer for compatibility (your vendor should have a link for this)

- Remind them to invite their friends and colleagues

This letter only goes out to those who have registered for the webinar. Make sure you're keeping tabs on your list. Thanking people who have no way of attending, or inviting people who have already agreed to come makes you look unprofessional and small time.

"THANK YOU FOR JOINING US" LETTER

Because this letter has to go out almost immediately after the webinar, you don't want to be scrambling to complete and proof it at the last minute. Take the time now to craft a "thank you" to those who joined you for the webinar. Whether it's hundreds or a dozen, these people gave up their time to listen to what you have to say. It's time for you to solidify that relationship, continue to add value and move the sales cycle forward.

This letter should contain the following things, in this order:

- A sincere thank you for attending the webinar, and a hope that they found value in it

- A link to the evaluation form

- A link to the premium, as promised (can also be an attachment to the e-mail)

- Notification that the webinar will be posted on your website (you might not know the exact link yet but you should have the page designed) and when it should be available if they want to review it or share it with their friends

- Your call to action - what is it you want them to do now that they've seen your webinar and learned what a great organization you are?

- Contact information. If possible; who is their local sales rep and how do they reach her? Who should they reach out to? If you're not working on a local basis, how do they contact you to follow up? (Because you know they'll be chomping at the bit to do so.)

Here is a basic template for a "Thank You for Joining Us Letter":

Sample "Thank You for Joining Us" Letter

Dear _____

Thank you for attending today's "5 Ways To Stop the Lithuanian Boll Weevil" Webinar. We hope you found the investment of time informative and valuable.

Because your opinion is valuable to us, we'd love to hear your feedback. Please click on the link below and answer 5 simple questions that will help us continue to improve our education efforts.

LINK TO EVALUATION

To thank you for your time, we have attached, with our compliments, (the premium you promised). We know you'll find it invaluable in your battle against these nasty pests.

The recording of this webinar will be available within 24 hours (depending on your platform) at LINK HERE. We know we covered a lot of information in our time together and this is a great way to review the content. Also please share this link with your friends and colleagues- anyone you think might benefit from seeing the presentation.

We at (your company) are eager to assist you in the fight against these pests. One great step would be to schedule a demonstration of our product. If you'll contact us at ———————— we will arrange for a personal look at just how we can help you achieve success.

Again, thank you for attending the webinar, and we look forward to being of service to you in the future.

Sincerely,

Sales rep or Company President

Contact information

"SORRY YOU WEREN'T THERE" LETTER

Just as you're going to send a letter immediately out to everyone who attended the webinar, you want to reach out to those who registered but didn't attend. After all, these people were interested and motivated enough to sign up - they obviously have some interest in the topic, if not your product or service (yet).

Just because these folks didn't come doesn't mean you want to lose touch with them. You should send them a quick note to keep you on their radar screens.

The "Sorry You Weren't There" letter includes:

- Recognition of their registration

- Understanding that things get in the way of good intentions

- They haven't missed out - they can still view the recording (with link as soon as it's active)

- Remind them of the call to action - you're still eager to set up a demo or have a sales rep contact them

- Thank them for their time and attention

Sample "Sorry You Weren't There" Letter

Dear ———————

Although you registered to attend today's webinar, "5 Ways To Attack the Lithuanian Boll Weevil," we couldn't help notice you weren't there. We understand that in today's crazy work world, things come up.

We'd like to let you know that you have not necessarily missed out on the opportunity to learn the techniques that dozens of people (however many showed up - people love to be part of a crowd) heard. You can hear and view the recorded webinar by clicking here (LINK TO THE RECORDING).

We at ——————— know the topic is important to you. If you'd like to see a demonstration of the world's finest bug zapping product, or even get some questions answered we are easy to reach. Please contact me/us at ———————

We know you'll find the recorded webinar interesting and look forward to having you join us live on our next webinar event.

Sincerely,

4 DAYS OUT

DRESS REHEARSAL - ALL HANDS ON DECK

It's 4 days until show time. Now is the time to do a full-on dress rehearsal. The producer, the presenters and at least one person who hasn't seen the content yet should be on the call.

Here's one person you might want to invite - the sales rep for your presentation platform. The more you are paying, the more personalized service you can expect, and if you are investing in the platform solely for these webinars, you have the right to get the benefit of their expertise. Someone with a vested interest in your success can give you great feedback and even answer technical questions should they arise.

Why are we suggesting you do this 4 days in advance?

- You may discover you are running long - or short. Either way you want time to make minor changes without having to stay up all night.

- You may discover the recording isn't working properly. You want time to call your platform vendor and find out what's going on.

- You will be less rushed come show day. You have other job responsibilities, and without the pressure of a dress rehearsal, you'll have more time to clear you desk and leave yourself undistracted for the main event.

THE DRESS REHEARSAL CHECKLIST

Task	Who is Responsible	Done?
Dress rehearsal scheduled and invites sent	Producer	
Telephony working and recording functional	Producer	
"Cycle slides" uploaded and running (if applicable)	Producer	
Polling slides created and loaded properly	Producer/Presenter(s)	
Other visuals/applications as necessary ready to go	Producer/Presenters(s)	
Rehearse announcements	Producer	
Hit Record	Producer	
Introduce Webinar	Producer	
Presentation	Presenter(s)	
Monitor time	Producer	
Introduce Q and A	Producer	
Role-play questions for presenters	Audience member	
Close presentation	Producer	
Turn off recording	Producer	
Copy Q and A log (if appropriate to the platform)	Producer	
Save presentation with polling data and annotations (if appropriate to the platform)	Producer	
Debrief the presentation	Everyone	

1 DAY OUT

FINAL REMINDER NOTICE

It's the day before the webinar, and you want to do everything you can to ensure that people who sign up for the event actually show up for the event. A final reminder notice should go out exactly 24 hours before the scheduled start time.

If you're pressed for time, you can resend the first reminder notice with the simple change that the event starts in 24 hours. (This will also help people avoid time zone confusion. You don't think this matters, but trust us, it does.)

There's nothing more to be done. It's almost show time.

FINAL TECH TEST

If your company or organization is experienced at using the web platform, then you might be confident in your technology, and that the dial-in information and recording will work as it always has.

Try it anyway.

SHOW DAY!

IT'S SHOW DAY!

The big day is here, but there's still lots to do, both before and after the event.

For the Producer: You bear a lot of the responsibility today. Take a look at the checklist that follows this page but don't panic! Many of these tasks can be done well in advance of show time.

For example, most platforms allow you to upload the cycling slides and webinar visuals, prepare the polling slides and other similar tasks well before show time - even days before. Make the most of that time to lower your stress level.

For the Presenter(s): Just as with any presentation, make things easy on yourself. Here are some tips for more effective presentations:

- Put your script in a 3-ring binder and stand it up beside your computer where you can see it.

- Use a headset on your phone if possible. Only use speakerphone if the quality is good and you are in a closed room, safe from interruption and background noise.

- Don't forget to annotate your slides to keep them interesting. Mark your script at appropriate places.

- **Make sure you have a glass of water handy.**

- Don't over-caffeinate yourself.

- Log on at least 20 minutes early to ensure good communication with your Producer.

- Attend to all biological needs 10 minutes before show time.

- Speak loudly and clearly. (But then you've had lots of rehearsal and feedback so you should be just fine.)

- Don't be afraid to use your hands and gesture just as you would in a face-to-face presentation. Your audience will hear the enthusiasm and you'll be more interesting to listen to.

- Don't say "That was awful!," or any other editorial comments until the producer tells you that the meeting is closed and all attendees have left the line. Don't ask us how we know, but it left a scar.

For Support Staff: You should appreciate how hard this has been on the Producer and the Presenter(s). Be extra nice to them - they're stressed out. Execute your tasks professionally and make the attendee's final interactions with your company pleasant and memorable!

SHOW DAY CHECKLIST

Time	Task	Who is Responsible	Done?
30 minutes prior	Log into meeting	Producer/Presenters	
30 minutes prior	Telephony working and recording functional?	Producer	
30 minutes prior *	"Cycle slides" uploaded and running (if applicable)	Producer	
20 minutes prior	Polling slides created and loaded properly	Producer/Presenter(s)	
20 minutes prior	Other visuals/applications as necessary ready to go	Producer/Presenters(s)	
15 minutes prior	15 minutes announcement	Producer	
10 minutes prior	10 minute announcement	Producer	
5 minutes prior	5 minute announcement	Producer	
1 minute before	Hit Record	Producer	
	Introduce Webinar	Producer	
	Presentation	Presenter(s)	
	Monitor time	Producer	
	Monitor Q and A box, choose questions, answer the easy ones	Producer	
	Introduce Q and A	Producer	
	Role-play questions for presenters	Audience member	
	Close presentation	Producer	
	Turn off recording	Producer	
	Copy Q and A log (if appropriate to the platform)	Producer	
	Save presentation with polling data and annotations (if appropriate to the platform)	Producer	
5 minutes after	Close the platform, end the webinar	Producer	
10 minutes after	Debrief the presentation	Everyone	
15 minutes after	Check on Recording	Producer	
30 minutes after	Send "Thank You for Joining Us" letters	Support Staff	
35 minutes after	Send "Sorry we missed you " letters	Support Staff	
1 hour after	Send premium (if not attached to the Thank You letter)	Support Staff	
Next Morning	Check and collate Survey results	Producer	
Next Morning	Divide leads between sales people- no excuses for not following up.	Support Staff	

THE DAY AFTER

THE NEXT DAY

No matter how successful the webinar was, the sun came up as usual and there's still work to be done. In fact, everything that's happened up until now will have been nothing but experience unless you convert those attendees (and even those who registered but missed the event) into paying customers.

Here are the tasks that should be done the day after the event:

- **Check the online evaluations.** Compile reports and see what the overall response was. Odds are it will match what your gut already tells you. Remember, many people won't bother filling them out and only the very enthusiastic and the really annoyed will write comments. Don't let either the good or bad news upset your equilibrium. Just take it and use the feedback to do better next time

- **Take the names and contact information** of those who attended the event, and immediately get that information into the hands of your sales people. Remember, leads go cold exponentially - a lead that's a week old isn't just 5 days older than a hot lead…it's 20 times less likely to turn into something.

- **Get the recording up on your website**…NOW. Remember all those people who signed up for the webinar but couldn't make it? You want to keep their interest level high and provide them with the webinar experience as quickly as possible. Plus, you never know who will wander onto your website and learn enough to become a hot prospect.

- **Monitor your website and the webinar recording.** Your webmaster should be able to capture the critical contact information of anyone who watches or downloads the file. Match it to your list of people who registered but didn't attend. Again, get those leads into the hands of your sales people in 24 hours.

FOLLOWING UP ON LEADS

As important as the job of Producer and Presenter are in this process, no job is more important than following up on the leads generated by the event. Depending on the size of your average sale, it only takes a couple of deals to more than generate a positive ROI (Return on investment) for all the time and trouble over the last 6 weeks.

Done well, this event should have more than made your Sales Manager happy. Think about what you've done:

- You wanted new leads, you got them.

- Every one of those registration leads is interested in the subject matter you presented, even if they don't know or care about your company. That's still a cut above the average cold call.

- The attendees are even warmer leads and you have a valid reason to call these people, even if it just to "see how it went."

- In a perfect world, some of these people have even called you by now, looking for more information and moving them along in the sales cycle,

- The number of people in your company's contact data base has grown, and will continue to grow with each registration on your website. That's got to bode well for future business.

The team has done everything they can, but closing the sale and turning these leads into revenue is in your capable hands.

Get out there and sell something!

DEBRIEFING THE WEBINAR

Once everyone has had a chance to recover, it's time to take a look at the whole experience. How did we do? Was it worth it? Is it worth doing it again? What have we learned?

There is some important data you'll need to have to properly assess and debrief the experience:

- How many people did we invite?

- How many actually attended?

- How many of THOSE were existing customers and how many were new to us?

- What were the audience evaluations like? What was the feedback you heard from individuals who attended?

- What has the response been to the sales efforts? How much money is in the pipeline?

With these numbers you'll be able to truly assess the success or failure of the webinar. Maybe you didn't have the hundreds of adoring responses you wanted, but do you have a couple of real new opportunities in the pipeline? Now that we know what we know, might we want to try a different audience or a different product ?

Remember that you set you outcomes at the very beginning of this project. Now is the time to assess your success. It's also time to take a look at the process itself:

- What worked well?

- What can we do better?

- Did we have the right people in the key roles?

- Which parts of the system didn't make sense for the way we work here?

- Were we to do this again, what would we change?

WHAT NOW?

Here's where we part ways, for now. You have gone through the "6 Weeks to a Great Webinar System" and used all the tools, checklists and best practices. Some of these things worked exactly as planned. Some weren't a good fit for what you do and the way you work at your company.

- Maybe you don't need three rehearsals

- Maybe you can get the visuals done in 3 weeks instead of 5

- Maybe you're going to repeat the same webinar so a lot of the work is already done

- Maybe the producer and presenter can be the same person

This system is designed to be a living document, not written in stone. Our goal was to give you the basic skills and knowledge to put on a webinar event.

To use a musical analogy, we've taught you the scales - it's up to you to play jazz. Change it, ignore it, use your own best practices and continually get better at what you do. We used years of experience and best practices to give you the ability to put on a solid event, but how you use it from here on out is up to you.

Using the skills and tools in this system, you'll be fine from here. If you'd like more coaching, training and tools, you can always reach us at www.greatwebmeetings.com. We'd be delighted to help you become even more successful and use the tools of the 21st Century to grow your business and do more than present, but to communicate and connect.

Sincerely,

The Greatwebmeetings.com™ Team

ABOUT GREAT WEBMEETINGS

At Greatwebmeetings, we think using web presentation tools effectively s a critical skill for managers, , trainers, and sales people. Whether you're doing a marketing webinar for 100 or a one on one sales demo, what determines your future isn't the platform you use- it's how well you use it.

We believe that the effectiveness and return on investment for any platform lies in the people who use it. Do your people have the presentation, facilitation and sales skills necessary to do more than simply present information, but to communicate and connect?

Check us out. Our services include:

Turnkey webinar coaching and solutions:

Our "6 Weeks to a Great Webinar" system helps companies get the most from their investment in webinars. Whether it's a complete turnkey solution, where we coach you every step of the way, or a simple "Mystery Shopper" review with objective, professional written feedback to help you identify your best practices and where you can improve.

Proven training programs:

Just because you have access to a web presentation platform doesn't mean your people are using it well. Learning the technology is only part of the task. Communicating with proven communication and sales skills gives you the lift you need to compete in today's market place.

- Web Presentation Basics

- Advanced Web Presentation and Facilitation

- Conducting Great Web Demos

No nonsense consulting:

Do you want to save travel costs and time, but don't know where to start? Maybe you have training content you want to convert for online delivery. Our job is to help you make sense of the new world of communication, prepare your organization and leave you to run your business. Ask us for more details.

Visit www.greatwebmeetings.com for free resources and more details.

For an appointment, call 866.491.5968 X702

125 Quotes for Whacking Weasels - Centuries of Wisdom, Motivation and Snappy Comebacks From the Cranky Middle Manager Show™

What would Napoleon say to the person who ate your yogurt in the breakroom fridge?

How can Aristotle prepare you for that next performance review?

Can Romantic poets help you explain why that project's 3 weeks late?

Managers can't always find the words to motivate their teams, demonstrate wisdom and keep the weasels at bay. This hilarious book offers 125 quotes from people way smarter than you to help.

It's full of the humor, intelligence and insight that has made The Cranky Middle Manager Show one of the world's top management podcasts.

A great gift for the whole team at work, or just for that manager who needs to know they are not alone in tackling the craziness of the modern workplace.

"I enjoyed this book immensely, and I believe you will too. Keep it somewhere close so that you can refer to it when things at work seem a little bit insane. Wayne's book will show you that, actually, you're right…things at work ARE insane." Bob Burg, co-author (with John David Mann) of The Go-Giver

"Wayne Turmel has written a book as wacky and fun as his podcast. As you smile reading his quotes and the snappy comebacks, you learn—which is what a book is supposed to do, right?" Jack Covert, CEO, 800 CEO Read

A Philistine's Journal - An Average Guy Tackles the Classics

What happens when an average suburban schmo decides to go back and read all the books he should have read in college? The results are both insightful and hilarious.

"…a hilarious study of the classics by a very funny man" Grand Rapids Press

Brushed up on your Epictetus lately?

Have you really read the Odyssey?

A 1-year slog through the classics of Western Literature resulted in this hilarious and sometimes insightful book. It's a combination of thoughts

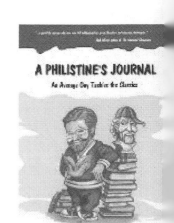

and meditations on what he read, as well as big honkin' samples of the books in question so you can honestly say you read a chapter of Robinson Crusoe, or Emerson's Divinity School Address. This book is the inspiration for the dedications and quotes on The Cranky Middle Manager Show.

Hey - people will think you're smart. Like, winning-on-Jeopardy-smart. You'll laugh and want to explore more.

All books by Wayne Turmel are available at www.crankymiddlemanger.com and Amazon.com

PRINTABLES

6 WEEKS TO A GREAT WEBINAR CHECKLIST

Purpose	To identify all the roles and tasks associated with putting on a great webinar
Who Should Use	Webinar producer, presenter(s) and support staff
Roles and Tasks	Webinar Topic: Webinar Presenter: Webinar Producer: Webinar Title: Webinar Date: Webinar Sponsor: Webinar Support Staff:

6 Weeks

❏ Agree on desired outcomes

❏ Determine Topic

❏ Determine Speaker

❏ Determine Producer

❏ Set Date and Time

❏ Investigate platforms

5 Weeks

❏ Get your data bases together

❏ Review Call to Action

❏ Determine title

❏ Determine data to be captured during registration

❏ Premiums and special offers

4 Weeks

- ❏ Finalize platform choice
- ❏ Schedule webinar in platform
- ❏ Create Landing Page for your website
- ❏ First invitation draft to stakeholders
- ❏ Draft of Registration Confirmation letter
- ❏ Script outline

3 Weeks

- ❏ 1st invitations sent out
- ❏ First draft of script to stakeholders

2 Weeks

- ❏ 2nd Invitation* goes out
- ❏ "Pretty close to final" script done

10 Days

- ❏ Plan evaluation survey
- ❏ Plan questions for Q and A
- ❏ Rehearsal!
- ❏ Edit, argue, finalize
- ❏ Premiums finished?

1 Week

- ❏ 3rd* round of invites
- ❏ Cycling slides*
- ❏ Reminder letter goes out

- ❏ Create "Thank You for Joining Us" letter

- ❏ Create "Sorry You Weren't There" letter

4 Days

- ❏ Dress Rehearsal

- ❏ Feedback and late changes

1 Day

- ❏ Final reminder notice goes out

- ❏ Final tech test (recording)

Show Day!

- ❏ Present your webinar

- ❏ Follow up with evaluations, premiums

1 Day After

- ❏ "Sorry You Weren't There" letter

- ❏ "Thank You for Joining Us" letter

- ❏ Check evaluations

- ❏ Post recording on your website

- ❏ Get leads to sales people

After that

- ❏ Debrief with the team

- ❏ Celebrate your success!

5 WEEKS OUT: WEBINAR PLANNING TOOL

Webinar Name

Stated Objectives

Presenter(s)

Introduction and Housekeeping (3 minutes total)

- Welcome, names of presenters

- Topic, expected outcomes, logistics including how long they'll be on

- Introduce technology, get them to try chatting, polling etc

Agenda and Polling/Assessment (2 minutes total)

- Introduce exact agenda for webinar

- Ask a polling or assessment question (depending on platform used)

Content (approximately 35 minutes)

- You'll want to use an inductive approach for most audiences

- What conclusions do you want them to draw?

- Why is it important to them?

- What evidence do you have (including your product or service)?

- Fulfill your promise to the audience for quality information

- Quick recap and ask for questions

Q and A (10-12 minutes)

You really want to encourage questions…this will give you a chance to remove objections, go deeper into the details than you could in the main body of your presentation and help you explain anything that could be confusing or get in the way of moving the sale forward.

- Explain how you'll take questions

- Start with planted questions to get the ball rolling

- Tie all your answers to your desired outcomes

Wrap-up and Call to Action

This is your call to action…why you're putting yourself through this. You'd be surprised how many presenters try to "wing it" or try to close too fast and forget to specifically tell the audience what the next step is.

- Summarize your main points

- Repeat action item(s)

- Thank presenters/partners as appropriate

- Remind the audience about the recording, tell their friends, fill out the evaluation form

THE DRESS REHEARSAL CHECKLIST

Task	Who is Responsible	Done?
Dress rehearsal scheduled and invites sent	Producer	
Telephony working and recording functional	Producer	
"Cycle slides" uploaded and running (if applicable)	Producer	
Polling slides created and loaded properly	Producer/Presenter(s)	
Other visuals/applications as necessary ready to go	Producer/Presenters(s)	
Rehearse announcements	Producer	
Hit Record	Producer	
Introduce Webinar	Producer	
Presentation	Presenter(s)	
Monitor time	Producer	
Introduce Q and A	Producer	
Role-play questions for presenters	Audience member	
Close presentation	Producer	
Turn off recording	Producer	
Copy Q and A log (if appropriate to the platform)	Producer	
Save presentation with polling data and annotations (if appropriate to the platform)	Producer	
Debrief the presentation	Everyone	

SHOW DAY CHECKLIST

Time	Task	Who is Responsible	Done?
30 minutes prior	Log into meeting	Producer/Presenters	
30 minutes prior	Telephony working and recording functional?	Producer	
30 minutes prior *	"Cycle slides" uploaded and running (if applicable)	Producer	
20 minutes prior	Polling slides created and loaded properly	Producer/Presenter(s)	
20 minutes prior	Other visuals/applications as necessary ready to go	Producer/Presenters(s)	
15 minutes prior	15 minutes announcement	Producer	
10 minutes prior	10 minute announcement	Producer	
5 minutes prior	5 minute announcement	Producer	
1 minute before	Hit Record	Producer	
	Introduce Webinar	Producer	
	Presentation	Presenter(s)	
	Monitor time	Producer	
	Monitor Q and A box, choose questions, answer the easy ones	Producer	
	Introduce Q and A	Producer	
	Role-play questions for presenters	Audience member	
	Close presentation	Producer	
	Turn off recording	Producer	
	Copy Q and A log (if appropriate to the platform)	Producer	
	Save presentation with polling data and annotations (if appropriate to the platform)	Producer	
5 minutes after	Close the platform, end the webinar	Producer	
10 minutes after	Debrief the presentation	Everyone	
15 minutes after	Check on Recording	Producer	
30 minutes after	Send "Thank You for Joining Us" letters	Support Staff	
35 minutes after	Send "Sorry we missed you " letters	Support Staff	
1 hour after	Send premium (if not attached to the Thank You letter)	Support Staff	
Next Morning	Check and collate Survey results	Producer	
Next Morning	Divide leads between sales people- no excuses for not following up.	Support Staff	